Necklaces

Soraya Feder

ISBN 2-914199-06-6

Table of contents

Introduction

Most of the necklaces presented in this book are costume or fashion jewelry. Industrially manufactured, they were created as a response to passing trends, with no real ambition to endure. They appease the desire for novelty upon the whims of the moment. The choice of a necklace as an accessory is intimately linked to the clothes ensemble. The ideal situation for every woman (and for jewelry designers) is to have a necklace or another piece of jewelry to be worn with every set of clothing, adding that special touch. The materials used to manufacture such jewelry are very diverse because their intrinsec value is not a criterium for selection. Their range is almost limitless, constantly renewed and diversified as technological progress permits new ones to be invented, or as more common materials are rediscovered and reappropriated to meet the incessant demands for newness.

In fact, the true value of costume jewelry is always largely superior to that of the sum of its materials. The difference between precious and fashion jewelry is a question of substitution and artifice. Precious metals – gold, silver and the platinum family – are replaced by more common ones, frequently copper and brass, which are plated with a thin coating of precious metal in order to improve coloring and resistance to tarnishing. Glass or crystal simulant stones replace diamonds, rubies and emeralds. What is irreplaceable is high quality craftsmanship for the settings and finishing in order to show off the design and the spirit of the pieces. These are the two most precious qualities of costume jewelry.

Enamel, amethyst, emerald and seed pearl necklace. France, 19th century. Jacqueline Subra Collection.

Enamelled gold, diamond and pearl necklace. France, 19th century. Jacqueline Subra Collection.

The reference to substitutions can however be misleading. Costume jewelry is not only imitation jewelry, the term reserved for copies of authentic pieces reproduced in non-precious materials. Ironically enough, while many precious pieces were often dismounted and their valuable components reused in more up-to-date creations, many pieces of 18th and 19th centuries paste jewelry have survived intact because it was not worthwhile recovering the stones and metals.

Although costume jewelry initially owed its existence to its more precious counterpart, the bonds between the two branches have become more complex over the course of the last decades. If the motto of precious jewelry is "a diamond is forever", that of true costume jewelry is most probably "dispose of after use". Nonetheless, the two are inextricably linked, for they share the same attributes of antique designs and sources of inspiration. It is necessary to add that costume jewelry is a vast domain embracing quite different worlds: from the worst-quality, blindingly glittering stuff to limited edition luxury and couture lines, executed by exceptionally qualified craftsmen with the best materials. Of course, most costume jewelry lies somewhere between these two extremes. We have added some precious pieces to illustrate how the two branches co-function.

Costume jewelry in France began officially in 1873 at the founding of their syndical chamber in Paris. Its development and evolution in the 20th century followed that of the major fashion houses. The couture jewelry lines launched by Coco Chanel in the Twenties, rapidly joined by those of the House of Schiaparelli, would prove to be the perfect stimulus for this art craft. (In

English, fashion and costume jewelry are synonymous.) Soon this sector would have two fatherlands, as non-precious jewelry prospered on both sides of the Atlantic Ocean, in France and the United States, two poles of creation and development as different as they are complementary. Despite its close relations with couture and ready-wear, where the brand or designer's name is omnipresent, jewellers remained more discreet. Until the 1950's, most pieces were not signed. Only a few large companies such as Trifari, Coro and Marcel Boucher contradicted this tradition. In France, most workshops were small or medium-sized and the pieces were produced in series which rarely exceeded several hundreds. The larger market of the United States allowed series reaching several thousand pieces to be executed there.

Above: Trifari. *A gilt metal and crystal necklace. Circa* 1940. Olwen Forest Collection.
Left: Christian Lacroix. *Crystal necklace.* Prêt-à-porter collection. Winter 1997-1998. Private Collection.

Crosses

Joseff of Hollywood. *Gilt metal and crystal cross with pear-shaped drop. Circa 1940.* Olwen Forest Collection.

Chanel. *Gilt metal and pâte de verre cross with pear-shaped drop. Circa 1977.* Olwen Forest Collection.

Solid guilloché gold and emerald cross. France, 19th century. Danenberg Collection.

The cross is one of the most popular forms of pendants. A religious symbol, it has also been, along with the heart, a common rallying sign among different groups throughout the course of history.

Since the Middle Ages, crosses have evolved conforming to all styles and fashions. They have been executed in all types of materials from the most precious to the most common.

In France, each region has its own specific traditional crosses. However, since the second half of the 17th century, the most prevalent ones were small Latin crosses. *Jeanette* crosses, as they were called, were simple or articulated, in gold, silver or enamelled, and were set with gems, pastes, or pearls.

20th century fashion designers included crosses in their costume or couture jewelry lines. Chanel, for example, preferred Byzantine crosses set with multi-colored stones. For Christian Lacroix the cross has become a leitmotif, along with the heart, in his Provence-inspired collections.

Normandy cross in gold and diamonds. France, 19th century. Mireille Jacquey Collection.

Silver, diamond and ruby cross. France, 18th century. Jacqueline Subra Collection.

Silver, vermeil and chrysoberyl cross. France, 18th century. Jacqueline Subra Collection.

Christian Lacroix. *Gilt metal and* pâte de verre *cross with* cabochon *drops.* Prêt-à-porter collection, Winter 1989-1990. Private Collection.

Diamonds and pastes

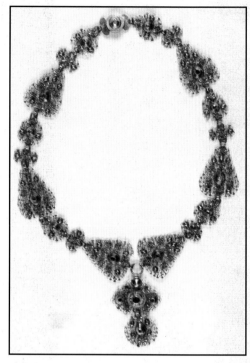

Gold necklace set with brillant-cut diamonds. Flanders, 18th century. Jacqueline Subra Collection.

Silver and paste necklace with cross-shaped pendant. France, 19th century. Mireille Jacquey Collection.

Diamonds have always fascinated. The name come from the Greek adamas, "untamable force". The most precious of all stones, it is also the hardest. Its capacity to capture and reflect is exceptional, especially once it has passed through the skilled hands of a diamond cutter. By facetting the surface of the stones, their sparkle is greatly magnified. Diamonds also have many other intrinsic values, and were already highly coveted throughout Antiquity. Cutting techniques were developed and widely in use in the mid-18th century.

New techniques for manufacturing simulant stones were developed to meet the growings demands of the nascent middle classes for lower-priced quality jewelry. Invented in England by Ravenscroft, pastes made from a mixture principally of lead and crystal, became socially acceptable and were worn by aristocrats who occasionally preferred beautifully designed imitations. The famous Parisian jeweller of this period, Georges Frédéric Strass, would do much to promote this type of jewelry throughout Europe.

The Virgin Mary. *Gold and agate cameo set with pearls and garnets.* France, Napoleon III period. Ouaiss Antiquités Collection.

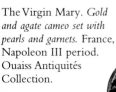

Multicolored agate and gold medallion. France, Napoleon III period. Ouaiss Antiquités Collection.

Cameos

Glyptic art, or the engraving of hardstone in relief or in intaglio, was already practised in Antiquity; cameos were highly prized by the Greeks and Romans. Cameos are low-relief sculptures very often using stones which are stratified in different colors such as onyx, sardonyx, cornelian and agate. Bust figures are the most typical subjects represented. A *connaisseur* of cameos, Emperor Napoleon contributed to the revived interest in these stones which would continue throughout the entire 19th century.

Hardstone cameos were very expensive and glass or shell imitations were less expensive alternatives. Softer and more easily sculpted, shell cameos were very popular during the 19th century. Cameos mounts were usually fitted to be worn as both a pendant and a brooch.

Pomponne gold and cameo châtelaine. Italy, 1820–1850. Private collection.

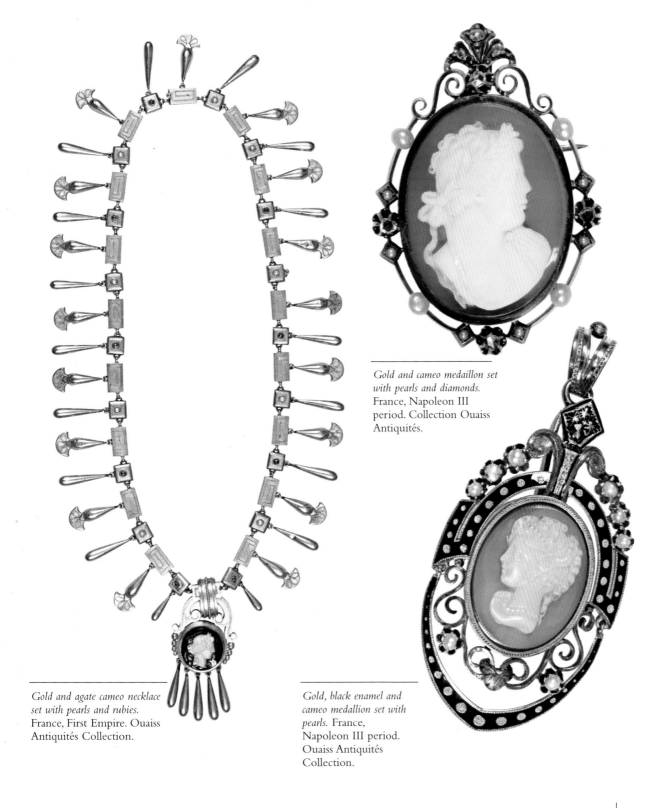

Gold and cameo medaillon set with pearls and diamonds. France, Napoleon III period. Collection Ouaiss Antiquités.

Gold and agate cameo necklace set with pearls and rubies. France, First Empire. Ouaiss Antiquités Collection.

Gold, black enamel and cameo medallion set with pearls. France, Napoleon III period. Ouaiss Antiquités Collection.

Pendants

Enamel and copper medaillon set with pearls and rubies. Napoleon III period. Ouaiss Antiquités Collection.

Silver and paste pendant. 19th century. Mireille Jacquey Collection.

Generally worn around the neck on a chain, the pendant sometimes hangs on a simple velvet ribbon. They were quite fashionable during the Renaissance. Often a precious stone was set in an enamel plate and surrounded by engraved mythological figures, or by a round or diamond-shaped plaque of finely engraved gold. The exuberant themes of the designs were inspired by the quite complex bestiary of fantastical creatures of the 16th century: satyrs, nymphs, mermaids among others. Large baroque pearls were standard elements of pendants. Gems such as jasper, crystal and heliotrope were utilized, mounted on richly engraved gold and set with a large drop pearl at the base. These pendants were usually worn on heavy gold chains.

Pendants of the following century were of smaller size and were more medallion-like. In the 18th century, pendants were worn with diamond *rivières*. Bow or flower-shaped models or those set with a pear-shaped diamond were highly valued by fashionable women. During the French Revolution, copper became the prevalent metal for jewelry. Jewels were considered as reminders of the *Ancien Régime* and generally condemned. Many pieces disappeared during these tumultuous times, either dismounted or melted down.

In the 18th and 19th centuries parures were often designed with a matching necklace and a piece which could be worn either as a brooch or a pendant.

Gold and diamond medallion with miniature painted on enamel. France, circa 1855. Ouaiss Antiquités Collection.

Silver, sapphire and ruby pendant. France, 19th century. Mireille Jacquey Collection.

Gilt silver and pearl medallion with miniature painted on ivory. France, Napoleon III period. Ouaiss Antiquités Collection.

Enamel miniature set with seed pearls and turquoise. France, Napoleon III period. Ouaiss Antiquités Collection.

Yves Saint Laurent. *Crystal sequin pendant* 1960–1970. Olwen Forest Collection.

Yves Saint Laurent. *Pearl and pâte de verre pendant.* Circa 1970. Olwen Forest Collection.

Yves Saint Laurent. *Crystal necklace with detachable brooch.* Circa 1970. Olwen Forest Collection.

Christian Dior. *Gilt metal and agate pendant.* Germany, 1974. Jessica de Ry Collection.

Silver and enamel châtelaine in the 18th century style. France, Napoléon III period. Ouaiss Antiquités Collection.

Gold and enamel châtelaine with watch and vinaigrettes. France, XVIIIᵉ siècle. Collection Ouaiss Antiquités.

Morel, Master goldsmith. *Silver and enamel châtelaine.* It *once belonged to the family of the Comte de Paris.* 1847. Ouaiss Antiquités Collection.

In the 18th century, superbly-crafted gold *châtelaines* were in fashion and would remain so throughout the following century. Including different useful implements such as keys, watches or the family seal, the *châtelaine* was worn at the waist or on the belt. *Châtelaine* models were specific to different French regions and, as part of the dowery, were thus linked to marriage customs. The implements on these *châtelaines,* especially those worn in Provence, alluded to the different wifely roles. Alsatian *châtelaines* of the early 19th century were composed of chiseled brass plaques evoking different professions.

The mourning necklace

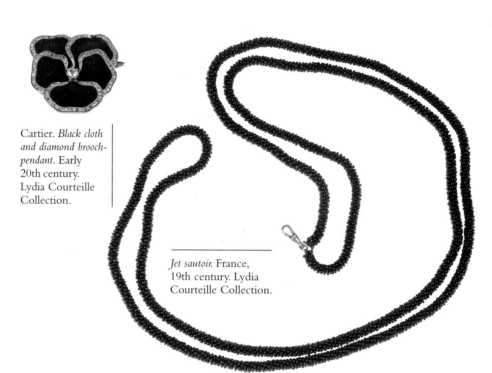

Cartier. *Black cloth and diamond brooch-pendant.* Early 20th century. Lydia Courteille Collection.

Jet sautoir. France, 19th century. Lydia Courteille Collection.

Jet necklace with heart-shaped pendant. France, 19th century. Jacqueline Subra Collection.

Although the practice of wearing special apparel to honor recently deceased family members is age old, black only became the official color of mourning during the 19th century. Strict rules regulated the mourning period for women, which lasted eighteen months for widows. They were in fact only directly applicable to royalty and aristocratic families but were observed by women of all social classes desiring to follow the example set by the privileged. Queen Victoria was the most extreme example, never resuming normal apparel after the death of Albert, her husband. She remained in black from 1861 until her own death in 1901.

Mourning for widows was divided into three periods. During full mourning, it was forbidden to wear jewelry. During the second phase, it was possible to wear white crepe clothing and black jet jewelry. The third and last phase, half mourning, announced a return to normal life and coquetry allowing a wider range of colors: lavender and gray were added to black and white. Fabrics were mat and the sparkle of black jet against them was even more striking.

An organic matter, jet is a type of bituminous coal used since Antiquity for decoration. An excellent quality of jet was necessary for jewelry. It had to be intensely black, hard enough to be carved and dense enough to be polished on the lathe.

Jet necklace. France,
19th century. Mireille
Jacquey Collection.

Jet necklace. France,
19th century. Lydia
Courteille Collection.

Parures

Parure is the French word for a matching set of jewelry designed to be worn at the same time. During the Renaissance, a *parure* was comprised of several different elements: a jeweled headband worn in the hair, a breast-piece which accentuated the bustline, a belt and of course a necklace with a large pendant. In the 19th century, with the rise of the middle classes and the development of techniques for manufacturing simulant stones, parures were widely produced and accessible to more and more women. After the Restoration, combs, headbands and belts were no longer considered part of *parures*. The word now designates a matching set of jewelry which may be as simple as a necklace and earrings but can also include one or more bracelets or brooches and dress clips. Many antique *parures* are incomplete as the sets have often been broken. The 20th century showed little interest in complete *parures* except for the period between 1935 and 1955 during which some sets using citrines or aqua-marines were produced. Since simplicity is the present watchword, complete *parures* are currently a thing of the past.

Gold and pink topaz parure. France, First Empire. Lydia Courteille Collection.

Following page: Joseff of Hollywood. *Non-reflecting gilt metal parure.* Evelyn Knapp wore the same model in the film *Wanted by the Police.* Olwen Forest Collection.

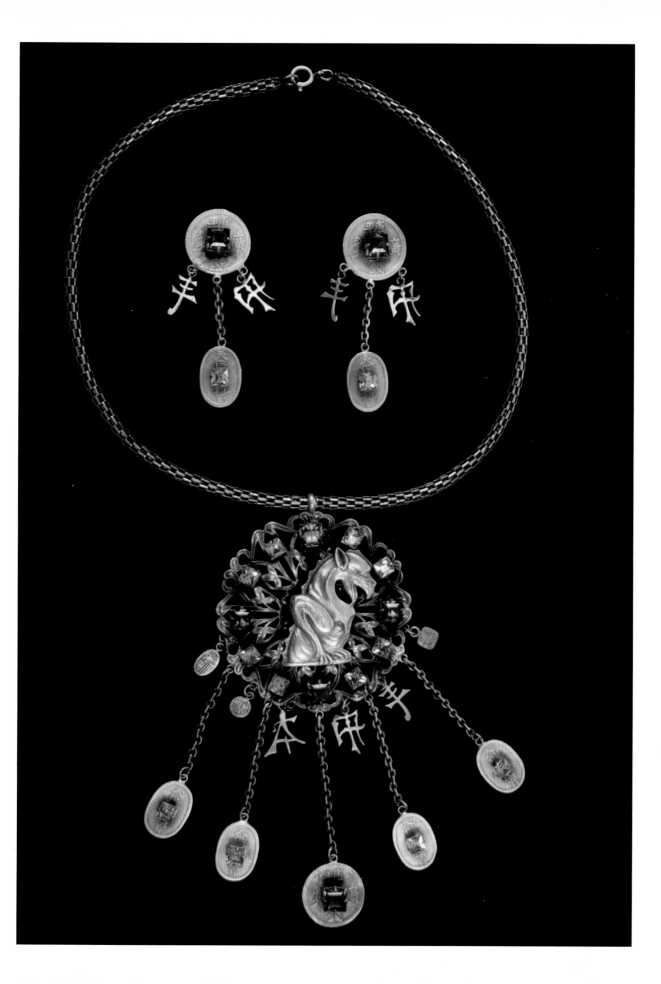

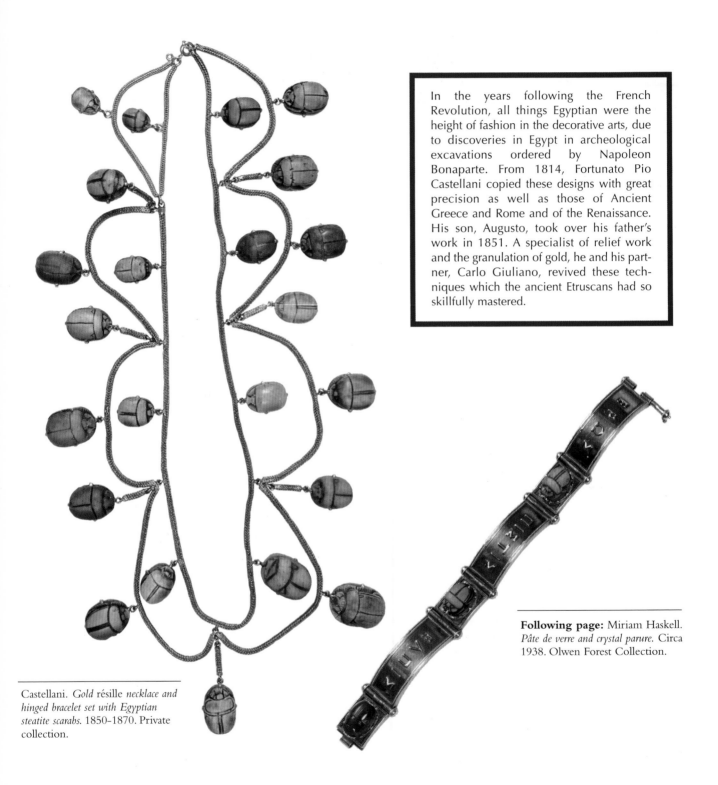

In the years following the French Revolution, all things Egyptian were the height of fashion in the decorative arts, due to discoveries in Egypt in archeological excavations ordered by Napoleon Bonaparte. From 1814, Fortunato Pio Castellani copied these designs with great precision as well as those of Ancient Greece and Rome and of the Renaissance. His son, Augusto, took over his father's work in 1851. A specialist of relief work and the granulation of gold, he and his partner, Carlo Giuliano, revived these techniques which the ancient Etruscans had so skillfully mastered.

Castellani. *Gold* résille *necklace and hinged bracelet set with Egyptian steatite scarabs*. 1850–1870. Private collection.

Following page: Miriam Haskell. *Pâte de verre and crystal parure*. Circa 1938. Olwen Forest Collection.

Previous page: Coro. *Enamelled metal parure with trembling flowers. Circa 1938.* **Above:** McClelland Barclay. *Gilt metal and crystal parure. Circa 1930. Olwen Forest Collection.*

Above: Florensa. *Gilt metal and pâte de verre parure. Circa 1950.* **Below:** Hobé. *Pâte de verre parure. Circa 1950.* Olwen Forest Collection.

During the 1940's in the United States, there were around nine hundred workshops producing costume jewelry and imitation stones. Most of them were concentrated in the Northeast, in and around New York and Rhode Island. Established in 1902, Coro (from Cohn and Rosenberg) was one of the oldest of these workshops. Eisenberg, who used Swarovsky crystal stones, Trifari, Hobé, Bogoff, Vendôme, Napier and Kramer were also premier companies. Activity would remain frenetic throughout the Fifties. Mae West was one of the first Hollywood stars to wear and thus promote costume jewelry.

Sautoirs

Bakelite sautoirs. France, circa 1940. Olwen Forest Collection.

Sautoir is a French term in use since the early 19th century designating a long necklace, usually decorated with tassels or pendants. In the 1860's, it was common for women to wear long chains with a timepiece hanging from them. In the Marseilles area, a woman would be presented with a *sautoir* at the birth of each child. These chains were mostly made of gold and were an outward sign of family wealth, although some were in silver or gilt metal. At the end of the 19th century, *sautoirs* were long, fine chains worn off the neck, over one shoulder and under the other, much like a military sash. This manner of wearing them brought to mind the extremely fashion conscious *Merveilleuses* of the revolutionary era and would be revived in the 20th century by Coco Chanel.

In 1910, thanks to the dress designer Paul Poiret, women adopted a new way of emancipated dressing, having liberated themselves from cumbersome underclothes and the constricting corset. Inspired by the Russian ballets of Diaghilev, Poiret designed oriental or Empire-style tunics in rich, fluid materials. He was one of the first Haute Couture designers to use costume jewelry as accessories for his dress collections.

After World War I, *sautoirs* were most often made of pearls and diamonds set in platinum. Changing fashions tended to more geometrical shapes heralding in the Art Deco style of the Twenties and Thirties. Nothing went better with the sleek ensembles of bobbed-hair, Charleston-dancing Flappers than long, rope-like pearl *sautoirs*.

Chanel. *Gilt pâte de verre sautoir.* Circa 1980. Olwen Forest Collection.

Chanel. *Gilt metal and pâte de verre bead sautoir.* Between 1954 and 1971. **Center:** Miriam Haskell. *Blue pâte de verre bead sautoir.* Circa 1940. Olwen Forest Collection.

27

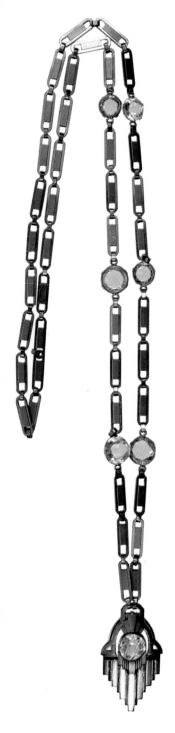

Left: *Crystal, silvered and gilt metal sautoir.* 1920–1930.
Right: Lanvin. *Pearl and crystal sautoir.* Circa 1920. Olwen Forest Collection.

Freirich. *Pearl and crystal sautoir.* Circa 1950. Olwen Forest Collection.

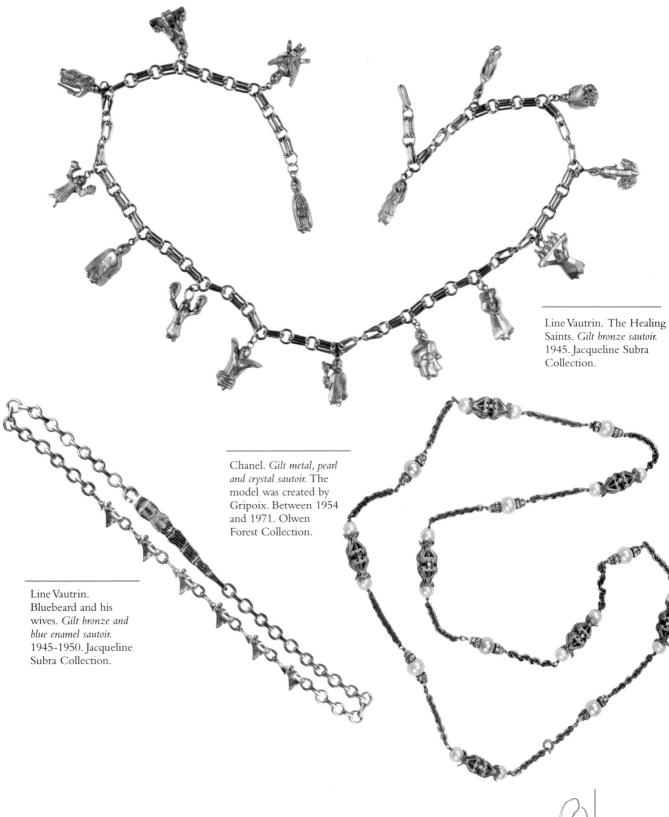

Line Vautrin. The Healing
Saints. *Gilt bronze sautoir.*
1945. Jacqueline Subra
Collection.

Chanel. *Gilt metal, pearl
and crystal sautoir.* The
model was created by
Gripoix. Between 1954
and 1971. Olwen
Forest Collection.

Line Vautrin.
Bluebeard and his
wives. *Gilt bronze and
blue enamel sautoir.*
1945-1950. Jacqueline
Subra Collection.

Gabriel Argy-
Rousseau. *Pâte de
verre pendants.* France,
1924. Galerie J. Point
Collection.

The Art Deco necklace

The Art Deco style would revolutionize the decorative arts during the Twenties and Thirties. Rigorous geometric and abstract forms dominated this reaction to Art Nouveau, the previous esthetic movement which had given precedence to arabesques and exuberant floral designs. However, some designers succeeded in reconciling these two approaches. For example, pendants created by Gabriel Argy-Rousseau borrowed fragile, translucent *pâte de verre* from Art Nouveau as well as its floral designs but their lines are more contained, tending toward abstraction. The chrome necklaces with bakelite pendants are more typical of the Art Deco Style, with big slabs of this synthetic material assembled in an architectural manner. Chromatic oppositions are strong and red, white and black are much in demand. They can be used together in the same necklace or each can be the dominant color juxtaposed with more subtle shades.

Galalith and chrome necklaces. France, circa 1930. Tiany Chambard Collection.

Page 32: Joseff of Hollywood. *Non-reflecting gilt metal and crystal parure.* Circa 1930. Olwen Forest Collection.
Page 33, top: *Pâte de verre necklace with metal balls.* France, Circa 1920. Via Antica Collection. **Bottom:** *Gold dog collar set with pearls and diamonds.* 1920. Danenberg Collection.

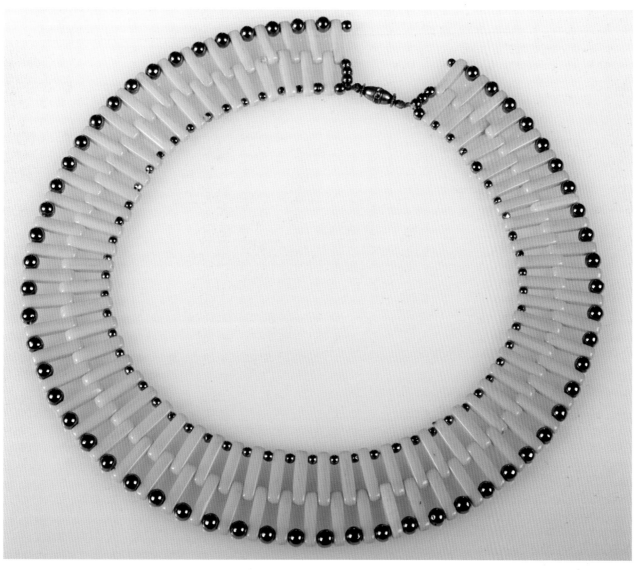

Chrome and pâte de verre necklace. France, circa 1930. Olwen Forest Collection.

Rock crystal and platinum necklace. France, circa 1920. Jessica de Ry Collection.

Jean Dunand. *Laquer on gilt metal necklace.* France, circa 1930. Ar'them Collection.

Jean Dunand. *Laquer on gilt metal necklace with silvered metal chain.* France, circa 1930. Ar'them Collection.

Interlocking chrome necklace.
France, circa 1930. Olwen
Forest Collection.

Gilt metal and black enamel necklace. Circa 1930. Olwen Forest Collection.

Bakelite and Galalith

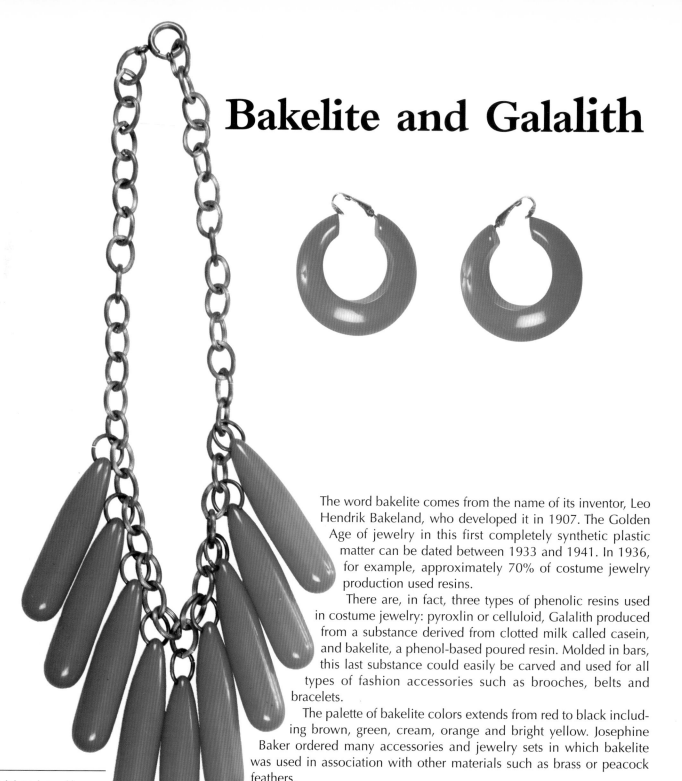

Galalith trinket necklace and matching earrings. Circa 1940. Olwen Forest Collection.

The word bakelite comes from the name of its inventor, Leo Hendrik Bakeland, who developed it in 1907. The Golden Age of jewelry in this first completely synthetic plastic matter can be dated between 1933 and 1941. In 1936, for example, approximately 70% of costume jewelry production used resins.

There are, in fact, three types of phenolic resins used in costume jewelry: pyroxlin or celluloid, Galalith produced from a substance derived from clotted milk called casein, and bakelite, a phenol-based poured resin. Molded in bars, this last substance could easily be carved and used for all types of fashion accessories such as brooches, belts and bracelets.

The palette of bakelite colors extends from red to black including brown, green, cream, orange and bright yellow. Josephine Baker ordered many accessories and jewelry sets in which bakelite was used in association with other materials such as brass or peacock feathers.

In the beginning of the Forties, new synthetic materials resembling the phenolic resins appeared on the scene. The age of lucite and plexiglass had begun.

Galalith necklace. France, circa 1930. Olwen Forest Collection.

Yves Saint Laurent. *Galalith and gilt metal bead sautoir on black cord, created by Roger Scemama.* Circa 1970. Olwen Forest Collection.

Egyptian-inspired silvered metal and Galalith necklace. France, circa 1930. Olwen Forest Collection.

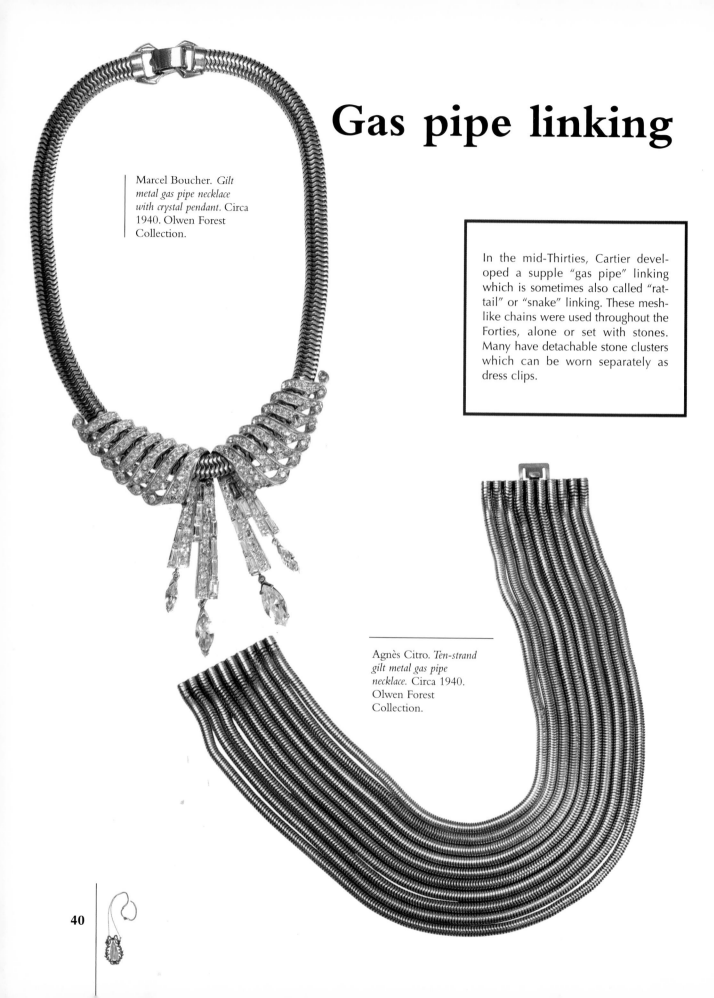

Gas pipe linking

Marcel Boucher. *Gilt metal gas pipe necklace with crystal pendant.* Circa 1940. Olwen Forest Collection.

In the mid-Thirties, Cartier developed a supple "gas pipe" linking which is sometimes also called "rattail" or "snake" linking. These mesh-like chains were used throughout the Forties, alone or set with stones. Many have detachable stone clusters which can be worn separately as dress clips.

Agnès Citro. *Ten-strand gilt metal gas pipe necklace.* Circa 1940. Olwen Forest Collection.

Six-strand gilt metal gas pipe necklace with disc-shaped pendant. Circa 1940. Olwen Forest Collection.

Joseff of Hollywood

Born and raised in Chicago, Eugene Joseff worked as an apprentice in an art foundry before moving to California. There, in the Thirties, he began designing costume jewelry for the film studios.

His intuition told him that the Hollywood studios were in need of authentic-looking costume accessories for their period films which would also photograph well under the strong light of the projectors. His parures were realized in a lightweight metal alloy which he developed especially for its non-reflective qualities.

He was correct. In the glorious years of Hollywood of the Thirties and Forties, jewelry by Eugene Joseff working under the name of Joseff of Hollywood was used in about 90% of the films.

In 1937, the success of his creations allowed him to commercialize a line of jewelry for department stores, completely separate from those he created for films. In fact, the studios did not buy his pieces but rented them.

Some actresses were very fond of his jewelry and wore them off as well as on the screen.

Following page: *Long gilt metal necklace with bell-shaped trinkets.* The model was created in 1946 for Joan Crawford.

Right: *Autographed photo to Joseff:* « With a heart full of gratitude to Joseff for his many kindnesses to me. Joan Crawford. »

Below: *Non-reflecting gilt metal necklaces with large tassels.* Circa 1940.

In a photo dedicated to Joseff, Joan Crawford is wearing a very long necklace of small metal bells. So taken by the piece and the tinkling music of the bells, the actress left his studios with the necklace, leaving behind her fur coat. Carole Lombard, Rita Hayworth, Barbara Stanwyck and Virginia Mayo among many other actresses wore his creations. Pier Angeli kept a seashell-inspired parure in her jewelry collection from the Forties.

The "Swing Buddha" line reflected the oriental influences in Joseff's work. The *parure* worn by Evelyn Knapp in *Wanted by the Police* is typical of pieces inspired by the Far East.

Joseff's renown was justified by his meticulous care for detail, and in particular, his filigrane work and interesting use of beads and crystal. Thanks to the finish of his metal alloy, his pieces were brilliant pastiches of fine Renaissance jewelry. Recurrent themes include sun, animal, zodiac and fruit imagery.

Page 46: Detail of the rooster *parure. Non-reflecting gilt metal.* The Forties.
Page 47: Animal–inspired jewelry sets: the bulldog and elephant parures. *Non-reflecting gilt metal and crystal.* The Forties.
Previous page, top: *Non-reflecting gilt metal necklace.* The Thirties. The same model was worn by Mary Astor in the film *Woman against Woman*. It was also worn by the young Rita Hayworth as shown in this photo. **Bottom:** *Snake parure. Non-reflecting gilt metal and pâte de verre.* Elizabeth Taylor wore the same parure in the film *Cleopatra* directed by Joseph Mankiewicz (1963).
Below and left: *Sun-gods parure. Non-reflecting gilt metal with trembling crystal eyes.* The actress Pier Angeli is wearing the brooch on her hat in this photo from the late Forties.

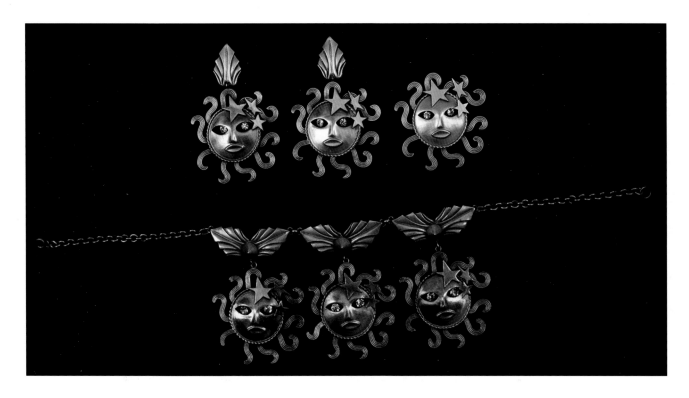

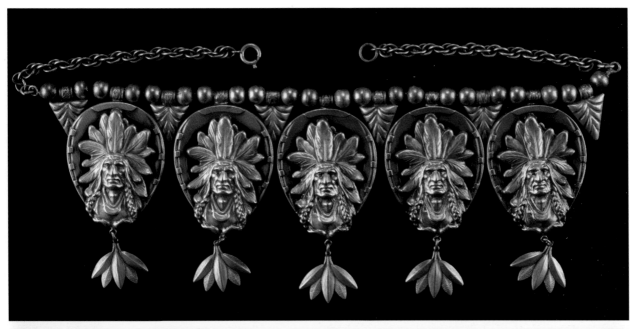

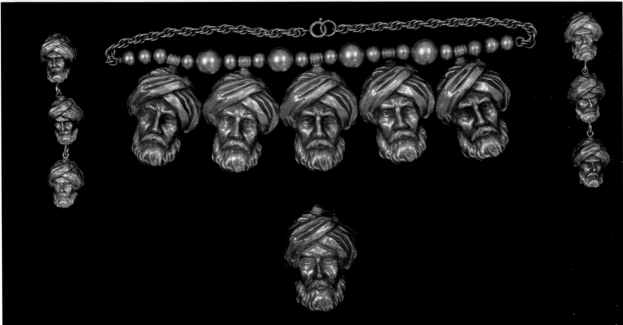

Previous page, left: *Non-reflecting gilt metal and pâte de verre cabochon parure. The same model was worn by Evelyn Knapp in the film* Wanted by the Police. **Right:** *Non-reflecting gilt metal sautoir with owl heads.* The Forties.

Top: *Non-reflecting gilt metal parure with Amerindians.* The Forties. **Bottom:** *Non-reflecting gilt metal parure with turbaned wisemen.* The Forties.

Gilt metal parure in the Art Deco style. Rolled metal was used widely in jewelry of the Thirties and Forties.

*The Calla Lilies parure.
Non-reflecting gilt metal
and crystal.* The Forties.

Gilt metal charm sautoir, created for the film *Fools for Scandal.* Circa 1940. The actress Evelyn Knapp is shown wearing it.

Other designers used materials similar to those of Joseff.
Above: C.I.S. Gilt metal *parure created for the* haute couture. Circa 1950.
Following page: Anonymous. *Gilt filigrane chain and trinket necklace with bakelite dress clips.* Circa 1930.
Olwen Forest Collection.

Elsa Schiaparelli

Shocking Pink *parure.*
Pearls and pâte de verre.
Circa 1937.

All the jewelry of Elsa
Schiaparelli in this
chapter is part of the
Olwen Forest
Collection.

Elsa Schiaparelli was born in Rome in 1890 in the Palazzo Corsini. She lived for several years in the United States, then later moved to Paris where she opened her fashion house. Its success would lead her to opening a second house in London.

Her first necklaces in 1931 were made with porcelain flowers, fur or feathers. She called upon the services of Count Étienne de Beaumont who had also designed for Chanel. Among her first pieces was the Egg necklace made with white beads and black laniers.

Originality and creativity were Schiaparelli trademarks as were innovative materials: ceramics, raphia, wood, rubber and Rhodoid. Throughout the Thirties, she remained in the vanguard of fashion; among her collaborators were such artists as Kees Van Dongen, Marcel Vertès and Jean Cocteau. In 1938, Jean Sclumberger imagined a necklace with metal acrobats walking along a tightrope. The artist and decorator Christian Béraud also collaborated on the Circus collection.

During the same period, she created perfume (Shocking, Sleeping, Shut, S le dernier) and jewelry lines with a bright fuschia pink usually present. This emblematic Shocking Pink became synonymous with her creations.

From 1937, her friend Salvador Dali directed her creations along surrealistic paths he knew so well. Giacometti also created for her house.

Shocking Pink
*parures. Pâte de verre
and crystal with satin
case.* Circa 1937.

Pâte de verre and crystal parure. The model was created by Roger Jean-Pierre for Schiaparelli in the late Thirties.

Attributed to
Francette Chapot for
Schiaparelli. *Seven-
strand pearl and crystal
necklace.* The Forties.

*Iridized crystal
necklace from the
Butterfly parure.*
Circa 1940.

*Iridized crystal and
pearl parure.*
Circa 1940.

*White crystal and pâte
de verre cabochon
parure. Circa 1940.*

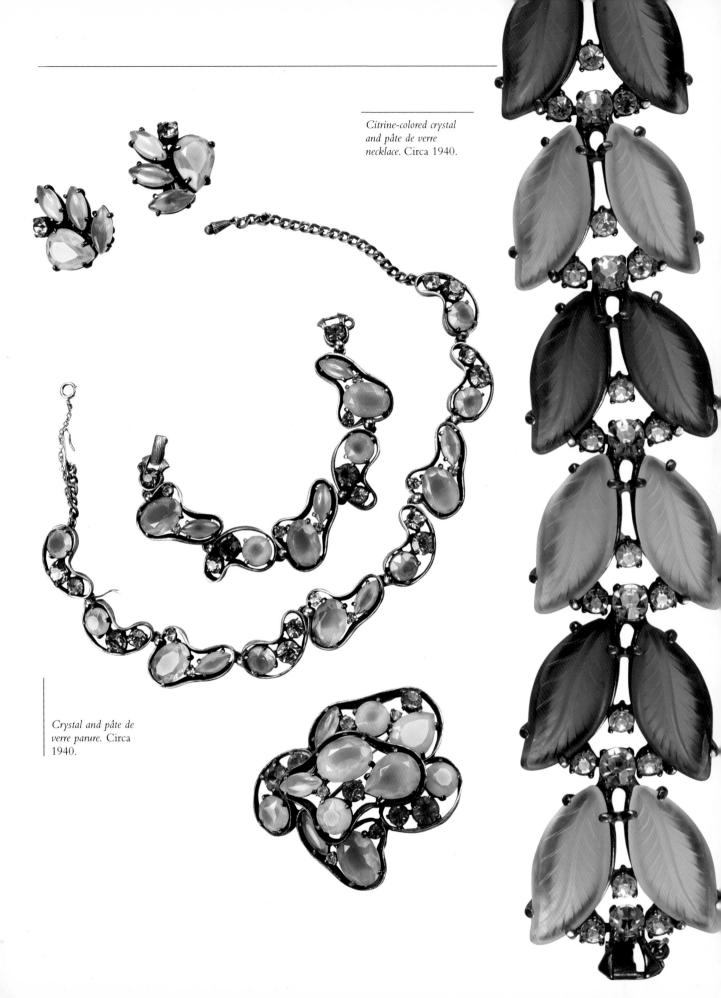

Citrine-colored crystal and pâte de verre necklace. Circa 1940.

Crystal and pâte de verre parure. Circa 1940.

Miriam Haskell

Miriam Haskell created her costume jewelry studio around 1924. Her first shop was located on 57th Street; ten years later, she moved to 5th Avenue. Great workmanship is the hallmark of her jewelry, as the pieces were produced on a small scale by skilled craftsmen. She had an inimitable way of using beads, whatever their size, in endless shades of color. Her sources of inspiration are far and wide: Greek and Roman Antiquity, African and Chinese ethnic jewelry as well as that of the Italian provinces.

Her creations attracted an international clientele such as Joan Crawford, the Duchess of Windsor and Catherine Deneuve.

Four-strand necklace with opaline and pâte de verre beads, pearls and gilt filigrane chain. Circa 1940.

Two sautoirs with gilt filigrane chain and pâte de verre beads. Circa 1930.

63

Left: *Pâte de verre bead and gilt filigrane chain necklace with heart-shaped pendant.* Circa 1940.
Right: *Chain necklace with pâte de verre and gilt filigrane pendant.* Circa 1940.

Gilt filigrane parure set with pâte de verre and citrine-colored crystal. Circa 1940.

Gripoix

Left: Attributed to Gripoix. *Grigri sautoir with multicolored* pâte de verre *charms*. The Fifties.
Center: *Gilt metal and* pâte de verre *sautoir with pendant*, created by Gripoix for Chanel.
Right: *Gilt metal and* pâte de verre *necklace*, created by Gripoix for Chanel.

All the jewelry by Gripoix is part of the Olwen Forest collection.

In 1924, Gabrielle "Coco" Chanel called upon Suzanne Gripoix, the head of one of the premier studios in Paris, to manufacture her jewelry. The craftsmen invented an exclusive technique for the fashion house, nacrage, which gave a mother-of-pearl gloss to pâte de verre beads. Between that date and 1939 (Chanel stopped production during the Forties), Gripoix created numerous pieces of jewelry, among them a line of Byzantine and Russian-inspired crosses, as well as the signature *sautoirs*. When in 1954 Chanel once again opened for business on rue Cambon, Gripoix continued to manufacture the jewelry lines. The Renaissance would provide the new source of inspiration for jewelry featuring pâte de verre beads and multicolored stones.

Between 1982 and 1993, the Gripoix studios manufactured many of the jewelry creations of Isabel Canovas.

Attributed to
Gripoix.
Pâte de verre parure.
1960-1970.

Pâte de verre necklace.
Circa 1960.

Roger Scemama

Far left: *Multi-strand gun metal lavallière with gilt metal plaque.* Circa 1970. **Left:** *Chain necklace and gilt metal pendant with imitation jade pâte de verre Buddha.* Circa 1960.

The jewelry by Roger Scemama in this chapter is part of the Olwen Forest Collection.

Roger Scemama collaborated with Elsa Schiaparelli in the early Thirties. A prisoner of war during World War II, he resumed work for Christian Dior in 1948. His creations often included stones from Czechoslovakia and many of his necklaces used oversized colored beads.

In the Sixties, Scemama designed jewelry for Yves Saint Laurent using popular stylish materials such as wood and plastic. His style remained quite personal throughout forty years of activity until the closing of his studio in 1975.

Attributed to Roger Scemama. *Silvered and gilt metal chain sautoir and pendant.* Circa 1960.

Gilt metal necklace with pâte de verre cabochon pendant. Circa 1970.

Roger Jean-Pierre

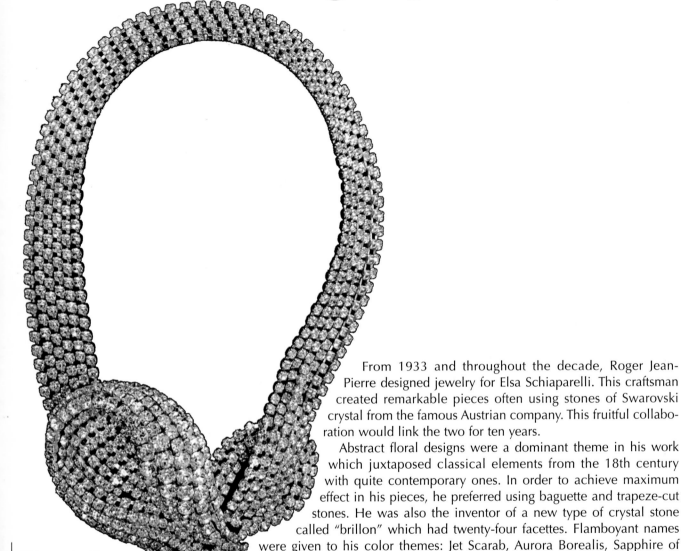

White crystal necklace created for haute couture. Circa 1950.

The jewelry by Roger Jean-Pierre in this chapter is part of the Olwen Forest Collection.

From 1933 and throughout the decade, Roger Jean-Pierre designed jewelry for Elsa Schiaparelli. This craftsman created remarkable pieces often using stones of Swarovski crystal from the famous Austrian company. This fruitful collaboration would link the two for ten years.

Abstract floral designs were a dominant theme in his work which juxtaposed classical elements from the 18th century with quite contemporary ones. In order to achieve maximum effect in his pieces, he preferred using baguette and trapeze-cut stones. He was also the inventor of a new type of crystal stone called "brillon" which had twenty-four facettes. Flamboyant names were given to his color themes: Jet Scarab, Aurora Borealis, Sapphire of India.

From 1947, he worked for Christian Dior as artistic and technical director of the jewelry department and would stay with the fashion house until Dior's death in 1957. He later set up his own workshop at the Place des Vosges in Paris where he created sparkling jet necklaces for Yves Saint Laurent and multistrand crystal and pearl necklaces for Balenciaga and Givenchy.

Gilt metal and crystal necklace. Circa 1950.

Crystal necklace and matching brooch. Circa 1950.

Previous page:
Crystal necklace, created for Christian Dior. 1961.

Above: *Crystal parure.* Circa 1950.

Line Vautrin

Necklaces in talosel inlaid with mirror. 1950–1960.

The jewelry by Line Vautrin in this chapter is part of the Jacqueline Subra Collection.

This designer was drawn to using certain materials such as metal, spun glass, ceramics and bronze. She opened her first boutique in 1939 where she showed her creations in frosted crystal and her white beaded necklaces on floral themes. In the Forties, her work was dominated by bronze jewelry. Her sources of inspiration were the sea, the lives of saints, legends and proverbs to which Line Vautrin always added her own personal touch of poetic humor.

In the Fifties, she abandoned bronze for a new resin-based material, talosel, which she would patent. This period was marked by limited edition brooches, necklaces and bracelets in talosel embedded with small irregular-shaped fragments of colored mirror.

Vautrin could easily adapt the same technique to decorative objects such as the looking glasses she created for the transatlantic liner France and for the restaurant, *Tour d'Argent* in Paris. Her creations attracted an international clientele including Marlène Dietrich, Brigitte Bardot, Ingrid Bergman, Yul Brynner and Françoise Sagan.

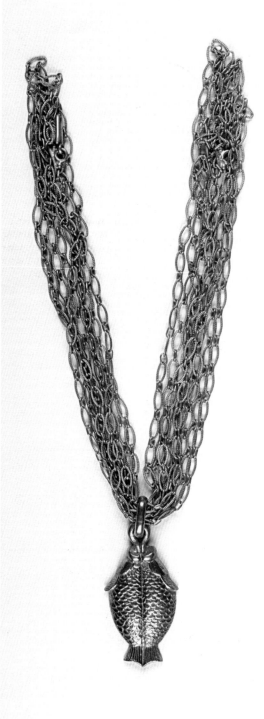

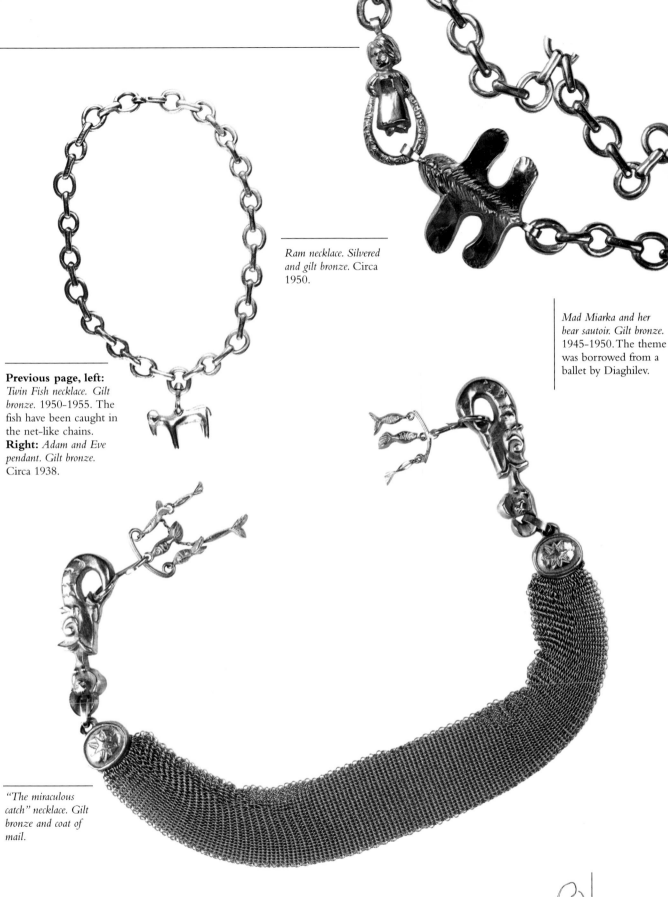

Ram necklace. Silvered
and gilt bronze. Circa
1950.

Mad Miarka and her
bear sautoir. Gilt bronze.
1945-1950. The theme
was borrowed from a
ballet by Diaghilev.

Previous page, left:
*Twin Fish necklace. Gilt
bronze.* 1950-1955. The
fish have been caught in
the net-like chains.
Right: *Adam and Eve
pendant. Gilt bronze.*
Circa 1938.

*"The miraculous
catch" necklace. Gilt
bronze and coat of
mail.*

Other designers

Isabel Canovas. *Necklace with twisted strands of beads, executed by Gripoix.* 1980. Via Antica Collection.

Trifari. *Gilt metal and crystal necklace.* Circa 1940. Olwen Forest Collection.

With the incredible success of costume jewelry since the First World War, some designers have made a name for themselves using very different styles and a large range of materials.

Founded in 1925, Trifari is today one of the most important costume jewelry companies in the world. Impeccable workmanship exemplifies its classically inspired pieces.

The Schreiner Jewelry Company is particularly known for its creations from the Fifties and the Sixties commercialized under the brand names Schreiner and Schreiner New York. Their pieces took form from prefabricated settings which were soldered together before being mounted with quality crystal stones.

Robert Levy, David Jaff and Irving Landsman founded Robert Company in 1949 later to become Robert Originals, Inc in 1960. Their necklaces are characterized by brightly colored beads and stones.

Lyda Coppola Topo and her brother Bruno founded Coppola & Toppo in the Forties. They produced collections for Haute Couture fashion houses such as Dior, Valentino and Pucci as well as for the own brand name. Many of their necklaces are composed of numerous strands of glass or plastic beads.

Kenneth Jay Lane opened his jewelry business in 1963 and his creations adorned the wives of several American First Ladies. Influenced by the Thirties and Art Deco, Lane adopted that spirit to his costume jewelry and used Swarovski crystal stones widely in his colorful and imposing style. His long fringed necklaces are often combined with dangling chandelier earrings in sophisticated *parures.*

The Kramer studios were founded by Louis Kramer in 1940. In the Fifties, he directed the jewelry department at Christian Dior where he designed *parures* in floral motifs using enamel, crystal and frosted stones.

Isabel Canovas followed along the creative lines of her predecessor, Elsa Schiaparelli. Her collections treated such themes as the circus, *gourmandise,* and animals.

Coppola & Topo.
*Seven-strand crystal
parure.* Circa 1950.

Kenneth J. Lane. *Pearl,
pâte de verre and crystal
bead choker with matching
bracelet.* The Sixties.
Olwen Forest Collection.

Kramer. *White crystal parure, created for Christian Dior.* Circa 1950. Olwen Forest Collection.

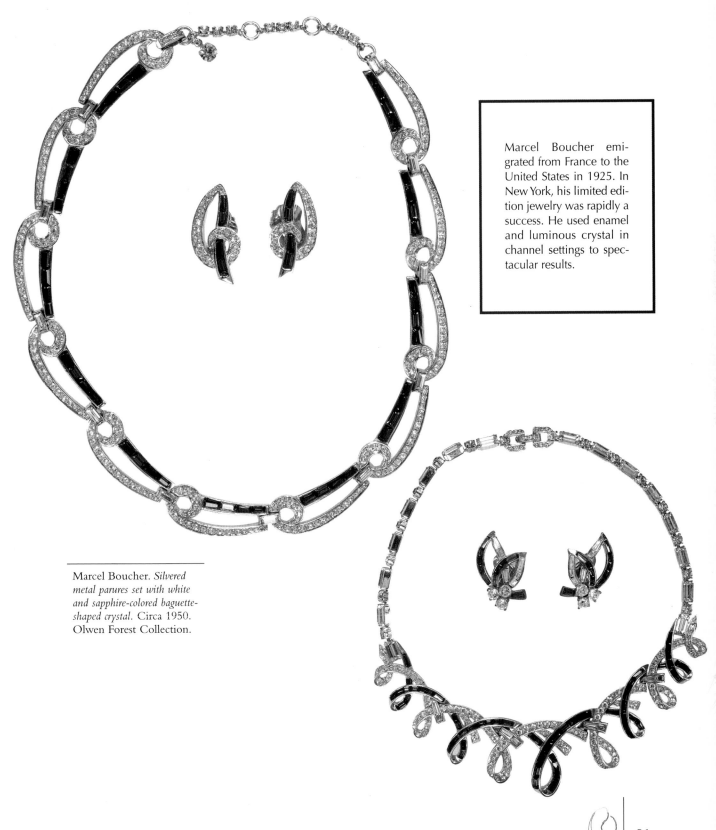

Marcel Boucher emigrated from France to the United States in 1925. In New York, his limited edition jewelry was rapidly a success. He used enamel and luminous crystal in channel settings to spectacular results.

Marcel Boucher. *Silvered metal parures set with white and sapphire-colored baguette-shaped crystal.* Circa 1950. Olwen Forest Collection.

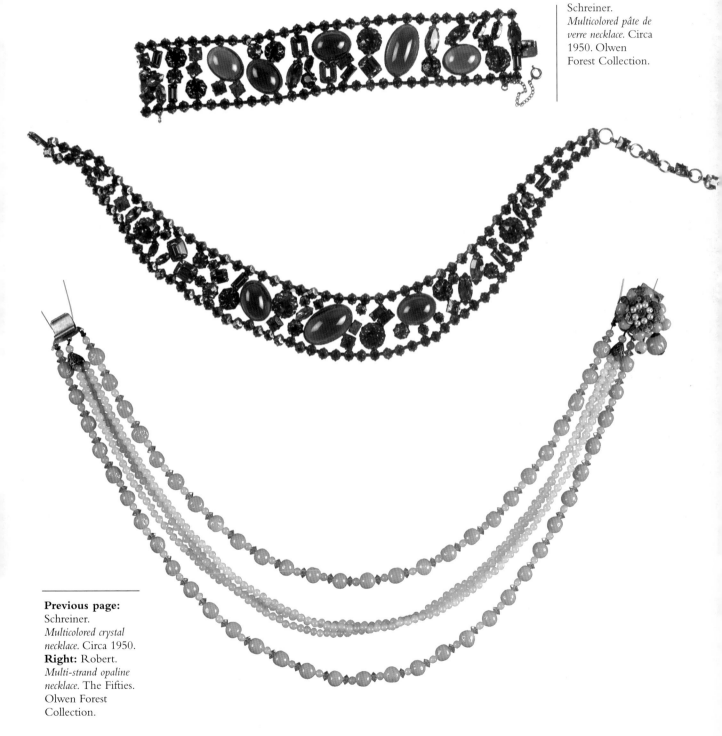

Schreiner. *Multicolored pâte de verre necklace.* Circa 1950. Olwen Forest Collection.

Previous page: Schreiner. *Multicolored crystal necklace.* Circa 1950. **Right:** Robert. *Multi-strand opaline necklace.* The Fifties. Olwen Forest Collection.

The Fifties

Articulated gold necklace and bracelet set with diamonds and rubies. France, circa 1950. The detachable pendant can be worn as a dress clip. Private Collection.

In contrast to the distinctive Art Nouveau and Art Deco styles, it is difficult if not impossible to define a sole style for the Fifties, given the enormous diversity existing in jewelry production. It is however possible to define the various currents which emerged in the course of the decade.

Among them was a neo-classical trend visible in many necklaces. Inspiration was sought in the ornamental designs of the 17th and 18th centuries. One art critic of the Fifties explained it in the following manner: "We are living in times which for historical, ethical and spiritual reasons are a continuation of the baroque age… This is particularly true for architecture, painting and sculpture." Jewelry could also have been added to the list.

Neo-baroque scrolls and arabesques were common elements in Fifties necklaces as were flower and leaf motifs. These patterns were often set in diamonds, rubies, emeralds and sapphire in platinum or gold mountings.

The bronze jewelry created by Line Vautrin in the late Forties and Fifties constitutes another trend of the decade. Inspired by themes from the Middle Ages, designs were deliberately simplified with heavy lines like those used in woodcuts.

Line Vautrin. *Gilt bronze cross.* France, early Fifties. Jacqueline Subra Collection.

Tutti Frutti necklace in yellow gold set with diamonds, emeralds, rubies and sapphires. France, circa 1950. Danenberg Collection.

Plexiglass choker with multi-colored mosaics. France, 1960–1970.

Chrome metal dog collar and pendant with acrylic tears. The Seventies.

The jewelry presented in this chapter is part of the Jessica de Ry Collection.

The Sixties and Seventies

Jewelry designers were captivated by new materials originally developed for uses having nothing to do with the decorative arts. This was the case for perspex, invented during the Second World War for fighter jet windshields. During the Sixties perspex, along with flexible vinyl, was reappropriated for decorative use in jewelry making. Laminated acrylic plaques would also be commonly used by designers.

A passage from a *Vogue* magazine article dated February, 1963 analyzes the contemporary styles of necklaces and pendants. "Jewelry is becoming more abstract, with less substance. There is no question of dethroning the grand classical pieces nor those little clips which have a story to tell (bouquets and animals). This is a new option along side of the two others. Abstract jewelry can not be ignored. These are objets d'art born from the imagination of young artists, painters and sculptors".

New materials gain in popularity: hardstones, enamel, stained glass, big slabs of colored crystal set in chrome, steel or silver. Scandinavian designers rehabilitate breastplates, torcs and gem-set pendants.

Chrome metal and amazonite necklace. Circa 1960.

Chrome metal dog collar and pendant. Fashion show accessory. 1960–1970.

Silver and cat's eye dog collar. 1960–1970.

Björn Weckström and the Lapponia studio. Space Silver Collection. *Silver necklace and earrings.* Finland, 1973.

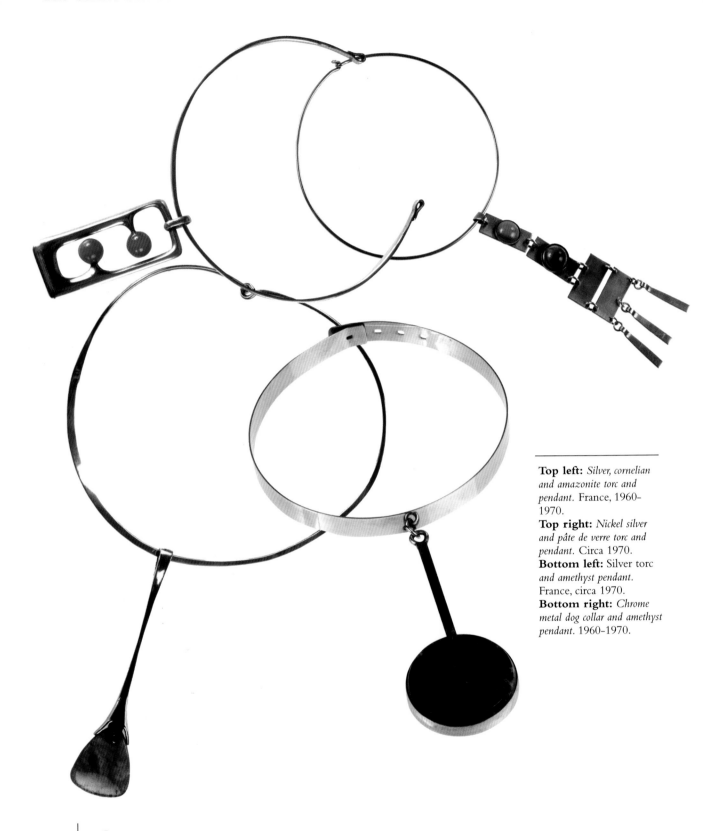

Top left: *Silver, cornelian and amazonite torc and pendant.* France, 1960–1970.
Top right: *Nickel silver and pâte de verre torc and pendant.* Circa 1970.
Bottom left: Silver torc and amethyst pendant. France, circa 1970.
Bottom right: *Chrome metal dog collar and amethyst pendant.* 1960–1970.

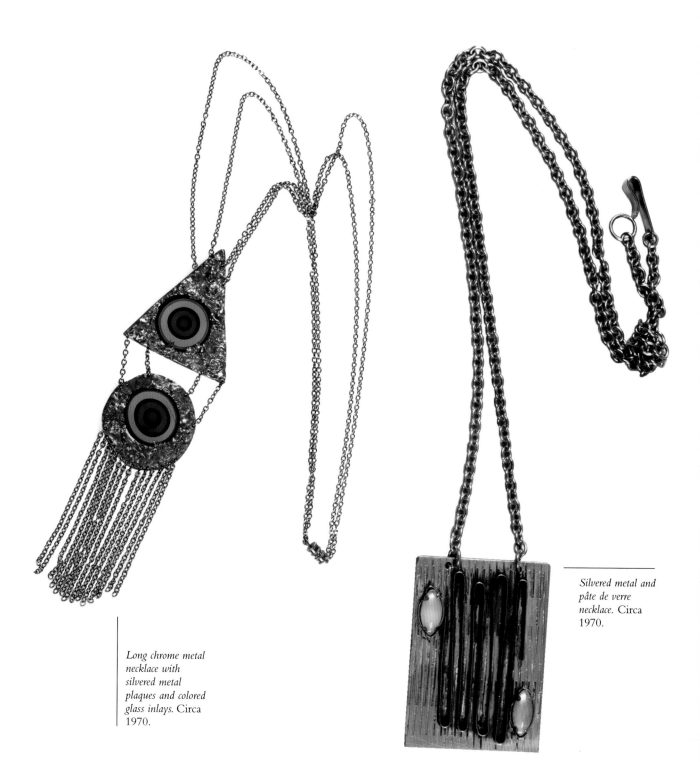

Long chrome metal necklace with silvered metal plaques and colored glass inlays. Circa 1970.

Silvered metal and pâte de verre necklace. Circa 1970.

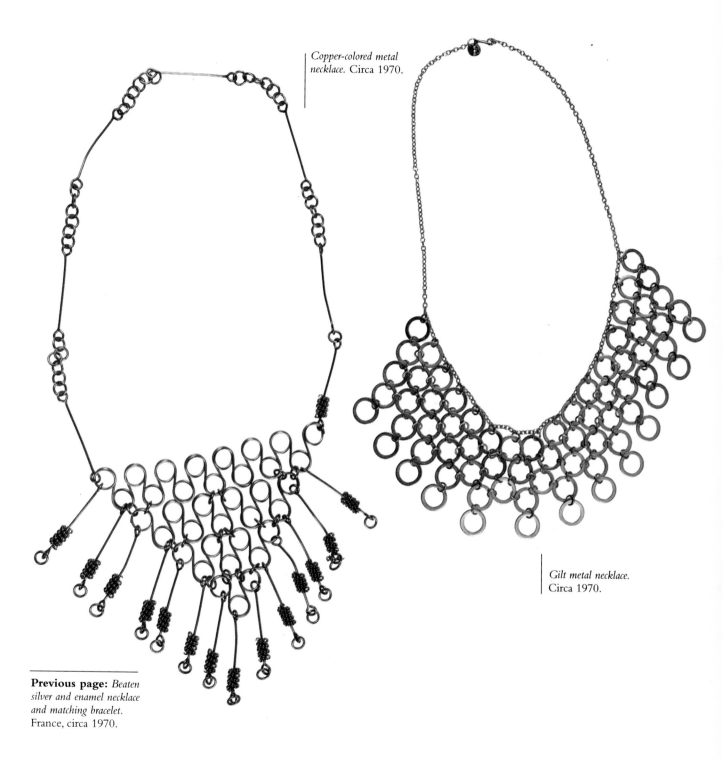

Copper-colored metal necklace. Circa 1970.

Gilt metal necklace. Circa 1970.

Previous page: *Beaten silver and enamel necklace and matching bracelet.* France, circa 1970.

91

Bibliography

Cailles Françoise. *Le Prix des bijoux,* Paris, 1989.

Dubbs Joanne. *Costume Jewelers, The Golden Age of Design,* London, 1990.

Gabardi Mélissa. *Les Bijoux des années 50,* Paris, 1987.

Greindl Gabriele. *Gems of Costume Jewelry,* n.l., 1991.

Hughes Graham. *50 000 Ans de joaillerie,* Paris, 1973.

Mascetti Daniela, Triossi Amanda. *The Necklace from Antiquity to the Present,* London, 1997.

Mauriès Patrick, Vautrin Line. *Line Vautrin: Jeweller, Sculptor, Magician,* London, 1992.

Mauriès Patrick. *Jewelry by Chanel,* London, 1993.

Mulvagh Jane. *Fantaisies: les bijoux chic et toc,* Paris, 1989.

Munn Geoffrey. *Les Bijouteries Castellani et Giuliano. Retour à l'antique au xixe siècle,* Paris, 1983.

Racheline Michel. *Bijoux et beautés,* Paris, 1987.

The author would like to address special thanks to Olwen Forest for her precious assistance. She would also like to thank Hélène de Struve, Jessica de Ry, Didier Ludot, Hélène Breton, Dominique Fallecker, Joan Castle Joseff and Le Louvre des Antiquaires.

Antique Jewelry dealers:

Le Louvre des Antiquaires
2, place du Palais Royal
75001 Paris

Jessica de Ry
Telephone: 33 1 42 60 00 85

Ouaiss Antiquités
Telephone: 33 1 42 60 56 99

Ar'them
Telephone: 33 1 42 61 54 22

Mireille Jacquey
Telephone: 33 1 42 60 18 56

Galerie J. Point
Telephone: 33 1 42 61 56 98

Danenberg et Cie
Telephone: 33 1 42 61 57 19

Tiany Chambard
32, rue Jacob
75006 Paris
Telephone: 33 1 43 29 73 15

Lydia Courteille
231, rue Saint-Honoré
75001 Paris
Telephone: 33 1 42 61 11 71

Didier Ludot
24, galerie Montpensier
Jardin du Palais Royal
75001 Paris
Telephone: 33 1 42 96 06 56

Jaqueline Subra
51, rue de Seine
75006 Paris
Telephone: 33 1 43 54 57 65

Via Antica
11, rue Jacob
75006 Paris
Telephone: 33 1 40 51 77 79

Olwen Forest
Allée 3, Stand 5 and 7
Marché Serpette
110, rue des rosiers
93400 Saint Ouen
Telephone: 33 1 40 11 96 38

Photographs: Robert Canault
Translation: William Wheeler

Photoengraving: Édilog, Paris.

Printed in Italy by Grafedit
August 2000